The Ten Commandments for Hockey Parents-

Lessons Learned by Breaking Them All

Melissa West Versich

DEDICATION

To my son Christiano- *I am so proud of all of your accomplishments. Thank you for being you- forgiving of so much bad behavior on my part, so loving and patient! You are truly "extraordinary"... Matthew 19:26- "With God All Things Are Possible." Hopefully, I can make you as proud of me as I am of you!*

To my dad- *Thank you for giving me the love and passion for the game of hockey, and for showing me how to hand that down to my son! All the State tournaments, trips and talks- you will forever be my connection to this incredible sport. I can see you wearing your Coach's jacket, pushing us all to be better. I will never forget your championship, and neither will any of your players. We are all better people because of you!*

To my mother- *my Queen- I know somehow, someway, you are celebrating this accomplishment with me. You pushed me to do something amazing, and not let my circumstances dictate my goals and dreams. I believe I passed that down to my son. One of your favorite sayings still lives inside me every minute of every day- "Never, Never, Never, Give Up!" - Winston Churchill. And to that I say, I won't...*

CONTENTS

ACKNOWLEDGMENTS

Thank you to the following friends who have been crucial in completing this amazing project- Claudia Mescher, Jodi Tower, Lori Kolden and Shannon Scipioni for proof-reading help, Ashley Willis for cover design and Marilyn Kaeli for manuscript editing. Couldn't have done this without you all! Thank you!

I. THOU SHALT ASSIST OTHER HOCKEY PARENTS

Some of my earliest memories are of Hockey. Funny, those are some of my only memories I have that are vivid! My brother played hockey from the earliest age, and I became a self-proclaimed "rink rat". Following my brother, and whatever team he was on, around the great state of Minnesota-the STATE OF HOCKEY! Crazy as this sounds, my brother's hockey dictated our entire household. There were five of us children and the hockey schedule ruled supreme! I was his #1 FAN!! I grew to love the game beyond anything I could ever imagine. The smell of the ice, the sound of the puck hitting the boards, the horn after the period, the screaming parents in the stands, and the feeling of winning! Back in those days, there weren't any girls' hockey teams. Hockey was strictly a boys' sport. So, I lived vicariously through my brother, pretended to be a real hockey player skating at the outdoor rink, and settled by becoming a hockey cheerleader. Thinking back, those early days following my brother around, really ignited my love for the game of hockey, and also spawned the craziness and bad behavior that would follow for years to come.

As most hockey families know, nearly every weekend from October to March is taken up by hockey! Weekends, playoffs, out of town tournaments, our family was no different, blankets in tow. I remember one playoff tournament when my brother was around 13. I had gotten my ears pierced and they were horribly infected. We wanted to win that game so badly that this outcome was certainly the only thing that mattered in my life. Going into overtime, I prayed to the hockey gods (or was it God?) I said, "If Ed's team wins, I'll let my infected ears close up." And they won! I went on to let my ears close and heal because you never mess with the hockey gods. Being my brother's number one fan also included detailed scrap booking, and of course having a secret crush on at least one player on every team he played on. It seems that hockey was connected to everything I considered exciting in my life, and this feeling continued into adulthood.

My dad also had a passion and love of the game that started in his teens. He served as head coach for my brother's teams when he played youth hockey. I really think coaching allowed him to live his love of the game as well. He had played as a goalie for his hockey team in the US Army stationed in Alaska. In 1974 my dad coached a team from Kelly Lake, Minnesota. At the time, Kelly Lake was a smaller town outside of Hibbing. It was the city playoff and championship. Kelly Lake was certainly the David of the entire tournament, and the Goliath was the city team, Greenhaven. That 1974 PeeWee team, coached by my dad consisted of a lot of misfits, players other coaches may not have wanted on their team, including my brother. This team of misfits under the direction of my dad won the city championship! After all these years, we still have plaques and the large championship trophy proudly displayed in our home. At 89, my dad has said many times that championship win was one of the greatest moments of his life! Yes, that is why we love hockey! My dad still tells stories about how he would smoke his cigar and chew the end of the cigar while coaching on the bench. He would then nervously pace and spit the chew on the floor of the players' box! He said once, "Can you imagine if coaches did that today?" I thought, no, Dad, because that would never happen! He would later attend 40 plus years consecutively of the Minnesota State High School Hockey tournament. Tickets coming in the mail every year! And, as his daughter, I got to tag along! Growing up, we attended every single year. No matter what- didn't matter what teams were there- we cheered for the northern Minnesota teams. Those teams such as Hibbing, Duluth East, Virginia, Grand Rapids, Eveleth, were always considered the underdogs. Thinking back now, I was blessed to witness some of the most incredible games ever played in Minnesota state boys' high school hockey history. Among them: Dave Spehar's unbelievable 1995 performance of three hat tricks, multiple overtime games, and there was the five OT semi-final game in 1996 when Apple Valley defeated Duluth East. We were there! I still have those programs from 1980 through the 1990's. Of course, my dad started attending the state tournament around 1973.

Fast forward to 1997, my son was born. I almost immediately knew he'd play the game, or I was going to try damn hard to strap those skates on him! He had all kinds of issues in the beginning. And, when I say issues, I mean *issues*! Almost like he didn't want to play. Yes, I am a horrible mom for pushing him. My brother-in-law once told me the only reason my son was playing was that I "shoved hockey down his throat." I'm sure I did, but I always justified it by saying- we are a hockey family! Being a single mom, I became the sole supporter of my son's youth hockey experience. Up at 5 am for the early practices, hanging at the rink with all the dads. He had issues with equipment, mouth guards, oh, and my favorite: he was afraid of the buzzer! He would freak out and leave the ice when the clock expired and the buzzer went off. And then there were his personal side shows! He went through a phase where he kept having to go to the bathroom during the game.

Not sure what that was all about; nerves I guess? And another one of my favorites-while the game was going on, skating alongside the glass and waving! Through all his chaos, the trips, the money, I hung in there. I maxed out two credit cards in the process. People ask me today, was it worth it? It absolutely was. Not because my son is still playing, but because of my love of the game, the memories created and what I've learned in the process.

So, this brings me to today. Why am I attempting to help other hockey parents? To make money? To embarrass myself, my son and my family? It's simply to share my experiences in hopes that I can save another hockey parent from stress, bad behavior, legal threats, and anger management classes. If I could do it all over again, I can tell you honestly, I would not be as stressed out as I was, letting so many issues upset me. Things like what team my son was on, what line, and getting short shifted during games. I have learned that no matter what happens, it's not about me; it's about my son's development and memories! Today, I would tell my younger self to focus on the two things that I can control- my attitude and my actions. And, I would encourage my player to focus on the two things he or she can control- attitude and work ethic. Simply because for both of us, these are the only things we can have an effect on. Everything else that happens is a distraction that ruins the pure love and joy we have for the game, and often affects our player's journey.

I often wonder how my upbringing and early passion for hockey created such a monster! Yep, I was one of THOSE hockey moms- not politically correct, or classy. Terms to describe me included loud, mean, crazy, rude, crude, loathsome, revolting, obnoxious, certifiable, and just awful! The yelling, complaining, fighting with other parents, getting drunk at out of town tournaments, and bad mouthing the coaches. Yep, that was me. I almost forgot bitchy and catty! I truly believe that my stress and need to control my player's youth hockey did major damage to my reputation, but also hurt my player in many ways. Thus, while searching for forgiveness for my bad behavior, I have created the Ten Commandments for youth hockey parents (and other sports) to encourage other hockey parents to follow them! And due to my checkered past, I feel I am uniquely qualified to give advice to the current and upcoming batch of hockey parents because I have broken all the Commandments! My hope is that you will follow them, or attempt to, and if you do- I know you will be able to relax and enjoy your player's youth hockey experience- and remember to trust the process!

NOTES/ CHALLENGES/ GOALS

II. THOU SHALT IGNORE THE BOYS' CLUB AND APPRECIATE VOLUNTEERS

One of the most important things you will learn during your youth hockey journey is that there are many things you can't control, but as we will discuss in this book, your actions are something you can control! One is the boys' club that often rules youth associations, AAA hockey or club hockey. The boys' club is often one factor that affects team selections and playing time. And, I will say, this isn't just in the hockey world. Growing up, I saw my son play little league baseball. And the so called, "Commissioners" had their kids on the best teams, and of course- dad made sure they got to pitch, play first and short, and develop, by playing in key roles. Dads coached their kid's teams and recruited their kid's friends to be on the same team. IT WAS THE GOOD OLD BOYS' CLUB! Dads living vicariously through their sons, dads coaching their sons, dads playing their sons in front of all other players, dads coaching all-star teams- getting their sons chosen- and then giving their sons extra shifts. When my son was in youth baseball, one of the dad-coaches told me straight out "Am I going to play my son more? Of course I am - I am the one putting the time in and carrying this bag" (referring to the large duffle bag holding all the baseballs and equipment.) Yes, I understand that most of these positions are volunteer and if these dads don't step up, there will be no team. I appreciate these coaches, but again- let's just call it- most are going to take care of their children first. Now normally, this wouldn't bother me, but it always did because I was a single mom. My son was raised without a dad from seven years old and up, so I felt insurmountable pressure to be both parents, and I was. Perhaps this was irritating because of my son's situation, but I also saw many mothers whose husbands barely knew how to spell h-o-c-k-e-y, let alone coach a team. These parents seemed just as frustrated by the good old boys' club. In youth hockey, you also have your dads serving as board members of hockey associations and pushing their own agendas and their kids. Oftentimes the moms serve as team managers, pulling strings to get their players on the A team. There is simply no way to get around it. Now, listen as I say that again: there is nothing you can do about it. I was recently talking to a friend of mine who is indeed in the thick of the youth hockey circles. She admitted that, yes, the boys' club does exist, but without these members or as she called them, "parent volunteers", there would be no hockey. As part of her argument, she discussed how some of these coaches put in 20+ hours per week. She blatantly stated, "If these volunteer/coaches/dads help out a team, and in return their player gets bumped to a higher team, I don't care, they deserve it!" Her most candid comment came next. "If parents want to bitch, they should volunteer!" She may certainly be right on, but this facet of youth hockey always made me crazy-don't let it do the same to you!

We must manage our emotions, which is something I was blatantly horrible at doing. And, I was also very protective of my son, and when I could see the boys' club frustrating him, it bubbled over! In 2007, we were at an away tournament in Winnipeg, Canada, and my son was on a horrible team. They had lost every game since the tournament started on Thursday. I was beyond frustrated! I remember being exhausted from the drive, frustrated by the losses, worried about the mounting trip expenses, and angry over the coach's obvious favoritism toward certain players. I knew certain coaches were close friends with certain dads on the team, and those players received the playing time. Let me clue you in on an important fact- frustration and anger do not mix well with alcohol. If you are going to have a few drinks (or more) do NOT attempt to hang out with other parents or coaches. After consuming alcohol, we all tend to overshare our feelings and concerns. BAD IDEA! After a wonderful dinner with a couple of my good friends, we headed toward the hotel bar after the boys went to bed for the night. I ended up spilling my guts and bitching about the coaches to anyone that would listen. My complaints focused on how the coach was good friends with a couple of the dads on the team, and he tended to play their sons more than they should be playing, due to their lack of talent. Here's a visual for you: me stumbling around the bar, and parents literally running away from me! I was so sick by the time I returned to my room, I thought I was going to die! I didn't sleep all night, and had to drive eight hours or so home the next morning. The next morning on our way down in the elevator, we ran into one of the coaches; he barely looked at me, which was unusual especially in small quarters, such as an elevator. In the lobby, I noticed a little pow-wow going on with the coaches and a few parents. I didn't think anything of it, really.

Then, during our drive home, we were in the middle of nowhere, and I noticed one of the coach's vehicles coming up behind us. Normally, this coach would honk or wave. As he drove by, I noticed his wife had her back to the passenger window, and they made no effort to exchange pleasantries. That was the second red flag. The third came about three days later when I received a letter from the hockey club with my check for the second half of the season. The letter told me that my son was no longer on the team due to my bad behaviors.

And I say that as plural. The letter was like a highlight reel of my bad behavior: yelling at refs, arguing with parents, swearing at opposing team's parents, and of course- my drunken outburst at the hotel on the hockey trip. The letter concluded with a threat. If I did not refrain from criticizing the club, they would consider suing me for libel and slander. My first reaction was to be defensive. "Whatever, it's all true. I'm just the first parent to say it." Then, the reality sunk in, and along with that, sheer panic. How would I break the news to my son? Where would he play for the rest of the summer? What would people think and say about me? After a couple of sleepless nights, I decided to tell my son what happened. I was honest with him about my bad behavior and apologized. He was devastated because he loved the coaches and his teammates. This was an incredibly hard lesson for me, but it was necessary. I wrote a letter of apology to the coaches, and they accepted my apology. My son was eventually allowed back on the team, but not that year. Remember, our behaviors and actions affect our players, and they don't deserve that. More on my bad behaviors in the upcoming chapters. So, yes I did it- I got my son kicked off a team! And, was threatened with a libel suit! And I deserved all the bad that came my way. Every year that I arrived at tryouts, I let the boys' club of dads and the politics, get to me! You don't have to. Learn from my mistakes and don't be one of *those* parents! Realize and recognize that this is a reality of youth hockey, whether your player plays in an association or a club. Unfortunately, there is someone pulling strings in some shape or form, and certain kids will appear to get special treatment. Expect it, and ignore it! I truly don't believe that any favoritism or lack thereof will affect your player either way, in the long term.

I have been called a helicopter parent, in hockey circles, "the crazy parent"! I bet you would never think of me that way after getting my player kicked of a AAA team! As parents, we don't want to hold our players back. If you get the reputation of the crazy mom or pushy dad- it could cost your player a spot on a team. No coach wants to deal with the crazy family- this coming from the ultimate crazy mom! Always asking why Johnny isn't playing more, and making up excuses for why Johnny isn't playing well. Believe me, I did it all. My player always seemed to be sick at try-outs and I always let the coach or evaluator know it. In the end- IT JUST DOESN'T MATTER!! Through my years of watching youth, high school, AAA or club hockey, at the end of the day your child will be judged solely on his or her talent and work ethic. The good old boys' club exists only at the youth, and possibly high school level. Eventually, coaches want to win, and there is an insurmountable amount of pressure to win, leaving them no choice but to play the best players. As parents, our job is to let our children know that, and not contribute to the problem by making bonehead moves like I did. Tell your player to keep working hard and good things will happen. Again, we can only control two things: our attitude and our actions. Our players can only control their attitude and work ethic. Trust the process! And follow this Commandment- Thou Shalt Ignore The Boys' Club and Appreciate Volunteers.

NOTES/ CHALLENGES/ GOALS

III. THOU SHALL ACT LIKE THE PARENT, NOT THE COACH

As parents, we often feel we need to coach our players, attending practices or watching from the stands, and taking mental notes to share after. And naturally, being the control freak parent, I gladly volunteered to coach my son in hockey beginning when he was four years old. Call it overconfidence, but I had been a hockey cheerleader and a figure skater (to some degree) and thought I would make a great volunteer hockey coach. At the first parent meeting, I volunteered to help on the ice with the dads, and proceeded to show up at the first practice. I was proudly wearing my white, 80's-esque Riddell figure skates. One of the dads pulled me aside and said, "Might want to wear your hockey skates next time". I laughed and said, "Ya, dah... couldn't find them this morning, so grabbed the old standbys." After the practice, I headed for the sporting goods store to find myself a pair of hockey skates. Found the perfect pair and was so excited to show them off at the next practice. BOY, DID I! I stepped onto the ice, skated forward and fell flat on my face! I was horrified! My son was even more horrified. There was another mom on the ice at the time coaching with her husband. She skated over and said, "toe pick". Red faced, and out of breath I said, "Oh yes, what an idiot I am". And, that was it. I had no idea how to skate without a toe pick. Well, the good news is, I was able to adjust to the hockey skates enough to fake it, but I never was able to gain the speed and versatility I had on figure skates. I tried the coaching gig for one more year, and by that time- my son decided to raise the puck and hit me in the shin. This started to become a regular thing. Yes, he thought it was funny, but by the end of the season, my shins couldn't take anymore, and neither could I. I needed to give up control of my son's hockey. I needed to allow someone else to coach him, and I had to learn to trust that he would actually do well and have fun without me right there. We are the parent, not the coach. And trust me, our sons and daughters will need us to be their parent. It gets confusing for them when we try and play the role of their coach. We, as parents, represent the safe zone, someone they can confide in and trust. If we start putting the coach's hat on, our player will feel they don't have anyone to confide in if they need to talk. Not coaching your child also includes not coaching from the stands! Yes, that was one of my specialties. Skate, pass, score! I was also big with the hand signals- the skate one, the hands up in the air as I'm disappointed. Keep your hands down! It is one thing to encourage your player from the stands, and it's completely another to yell …. For example, "Pass the puck" is probably you attempting to coach your player from the stands. "Good hustle, Suzie" sounds like you're encouraging them. There is a difference. Trying to coach other players from the stands is really a NO-NO. If you are anything like I was, it is best to sit far away from other parents or tape your mouth shut. During one particular game, my coaching from the stands nearly got me a cell at the local police department. It was the first game of a AAA tournament, and everyone was so excited with anticipation for the team. They had been practicing hard and were getting better. We knew they had the talent and work ethic to win this tournament.

The first game began with me on my best behavior as usual. I was in the stands screaming at my son, "Hustle, skate, PASS THE PUCK!" One of the moms on our team seemed irritated by my ranting and screaming. She kept staring at me during my rants. The more I screamed, the more her facial expressions went south. She then started leaning over, pointing at me, and whispering to another mom. That put me over the edge! I looked at her and yelled, "What's your problem?" She turned her head and didn't say anything. After the period was over, I caught her down by the bathrooms. I asked her again, "What's your problem?" She said something about my yelling not helping the boys playing well. I said, "No, they are not, they need to hustle to the puck, and win the puck battles." Things escalated, and I ended up using the F-word in some capacity. Another one of my proud hockey mom moments, coaching from the stands, and then arguing with yet another parent. In all my years of being a hockey mom, I can't even imagine how many times I embarrassed my player - both on, and off the ice. Thinking back, he never asked me to stop any of my bad behaviors. I think he figured that was me, passionate and crazy, always having his back, so he put up with me. Looking back, I wish I could take it all back, and realize that getting stressed out and angry doesn't help me, or my player. I can't control or change most things. I can only control my attitude and my actions.

Another one of my favorite methods of coaching my son was to be sure he got fair playing time. I didn't have a stop watch, but I sure knew how long he was on the ice compared to other players, and I wasn't afraid to complain about it. I realize that it's not fair when your player gets short shifted, and it's not fair when your child sits on the bench. I have experienced the anger and frustration from the stands. One of the worst experiences I dealt with was when my son was chosen to play in one of the Elite tournaments. As a parent, when you get that call or email, you are bursting with pride. They only pick the best players for those ELITE tournaments, right? So my player must be exceptional. After paying several hundred dollars, your player has yet another jersey she or he will never wear again, and often times, barely see the ice. At this particular tournament, I watched as game after game my son went out on the ice for a very short shift, and went back to his spot on the bench riding the pine. Followed by the coach's son playing around a three minute shift, power plays, and penalty kills. I was furious and so sad. My son got into the car with his medal and said how bummed he was that he didn't get to play much. I told him that it didn't matter. I asked if he had fun, and he said he would have had more fun if he could have played. All I can tell you is, this particular coach's son never played hockey past high school. Just remember: it doesn't matter. I know it's easy to say now, but it's true! If your player has the talent and the work ethic, he or she will play and do well. No coach, no other parent, no advisor, no short shifting, no snubbing by anyone can stop that, but, you can! Stay positive and focus on the two things you can control- your attitude and your actions. And continue to encourage your player to control what he or she can control: attitude and work ethic!

Finally, we have the coaching on the car ride home scenario. Studies show that one of the things kids dread the most is the ride home. Often it's the yelling, screaming and telling them all they did wrong. I couldn't wait for my son to get into the car so I could coach him, and ask questions like, "Why didn't the coach play your line?" "Why did he leave Johnny out there when he gave up all those goals?" Some of my other favorites include, "You need to work harder out there." "Why don't you shoot the puck more, you always pass!" One time my mom was in town for the weekend, and I was so excited for her to watch my son play in a tournament. As the game progressed, he looked like he simply didn't care to be there. No hustle, no care factor, just extremely lazy. On the ride home, I couldn't wait to dig into him. I told him if he didn't start working hard, I was taking him out of hockey. I went on to guilt him about how much money the sport costs, and how hard I had to work to give him that chance. My ramble continued with "You better do something out there, or this is your last weekend of play." Yes, it sounds horrible, and believe me, writing it feels horrible. I sound like a horrible person, but it was all about me! Not him. The worst part was that my mom was devastated by the way I spoke to my son. She immediately stood up for him, and told me that I was out of line. She was right, even though I'm not sure that I realized it that quickly. There is so much pressure in this game, and we as parents often take on that pressure and put it back on our players. I don't think in all my years as a youth hockey parent, I ever focused on having fun, and enjoying my son play, and that is just wrong! Remember, your child needs you to be the parent, not the coach. If I could do it all over again, I would wait and see what my player said once he or she got into the car. Would he or she start a conversation, and if so, would it be about the game? If he or she does, then go with it. I would be a much better listener. I will discuss this more later. It's better to understand our players by saying "yes, okay", and then focusing on the positives about the game, and my player's play. As parents, we need to remember to focus on our two basics: our attitude and our actions, and try to encourage our players by reminding them to stay with their two areas, attitude and work ethic! Tell them keep working hard and good things will happen, and trust the process! And, follow this Commandment- Thou Shalt Act Like the Parent, Not the Coach.

NOTES/ CHALLENGES/ GOALS

IV. THOU SHALT REMEMBER THOU ART THE PARENT, NOT THE CHILD

If you think about the meaning of hockey politics, it really can't be specifically defined. The way I would define it is BAD BEHAVIOR that potentially ruins the hockey experience for our players. I had ugly exchanges with a number of individuals during the youth hockey season every year such as referees, coaches, other parents, etc. We often don't realize that our bad behavior affects our players, and often prevents them from being successful. Yelling at referees was always part of a typical game for us. If the refs were calling the game in our favor, all was good. But when our team started getting the bad calls and penalties, I started yelling at the refs. I will tell you that this came to an abrupt end when my son was old enough to ref a game himself. He came home and said, "Those parents are just awful and mean, I don't care if I ever ref again." He went on to say he was so uncomfortable, he was almost fearful. This was a wake-up call for me. Even in the later years of youth hockey, we need to realize referees and linesmen are human. They do make mistakes and often miss calls and make bad calls. THEY ARE HUMAN! We need to allow them to make mistakes and forgive them. Unless it's the Olympics of youth hockey, we really are over-reacting by screaming at a ref. Especially youth game refs. If you look around, many of the youth game referees are kids themselves. Being a referee is not a fun job, so we should be thankful that we have individuals willing to take on that challenge. Remember before you scream at a ref, think about how you would act if your son or daughter was wearing the stripes.

Parent cliques can also lead to bad behavior from parents. Nearly every year, I had my inner circle of parents that I traveled with and hung out with. This isn't usually an issue being part of a parent clique, but it can become detrimental when we start creating an adversarial relationship with other parent groups and their players. As parents, we don't always realize that our kids are listening. They know the parents we like on our teams, and the ones we don't. They have heard us complain about Johnny and his crazy mom. One car ride home after a game, my son was riding the back seat with one of his teammates. They started talking about the game, and criticizing a couple of the players on their team. Well, it just so happened that these players were children of my least favorite parents. Yes, my son had been listening to me bad mouthing these players and their parents, and now he was doing the same. This made for a very difficult couple years of hockey. The situation continued to get worse as we had a group of four to five parents in one group, and another group with an equal number. Our parent groups didn't get along, and as a result, neither did our players. There was a line drawn right down the middle: Us –vs-Them. I remember at one of our away tournaments in Wisconsin, our team was a late addition and as a result, the team and parents had to stay at two separate hotels. Predictably, the cliques of players and parents stayed together in the same hotel. It was strange as everyone would show up at the games, so it seemed we were on different teams. Parent cliques just don't belong in youth hockey. These cliques definitely create the biggest challenges for the coaches. The players ended up never trusting or liking each other, and this often spilled over during practices. Although we had a very talented team that year, we never did make the state tournament. The sad part is at the time, I didn't see that I was doing anything wrong. I was protecting my son, and being territorial about who I considered a good person in the parent department. Truth is, we have no business judging other parents or kids. In order to keep the peace on the team, as parents, we need to lead by example. I found myself most of the time acting like the kid, and my kid was acting like the parent. Did I just say that? Yes, I did, and it's all true. Our kids are watching us, and they are listening. If you can't say anything nice, be quiet!

During the same tournament in Wisconsin, my bad behavior once again took center stage. Following a game that we won in OT, my son was acting like an idiot on the ice. He was taunting the other players and fans. It was not a proud moment for me, but I definitely made the situation worse by trying to protect him. One of the moms from our team came up to me in the lobby afterwards and said, "I don't think your son conducted himself very well out there tonight." She barely got another word out of her mouth and I totally attacked her. My mama bear mentality went into protection mode, and I let her have it with everything I had. I could feel the anger and rage rising up in me. I screamed at her, asking her who the hell she thought she was judging my son, and her son wasn't perfect. This argument continued into the parking lot. Yes, another one of my proud hockey mom moments. The sad part about the exchange was once again, the entire team and coaches found out about the event, and it was an event! I embarrassed my son, and ruined my relationship with this mom and several other parents on the team. Was she out of line? Yes, I think she was, but again, I made things worse by coming unglued. I have said it a myriad of times and I will continue to say it... as parents, we can only control our attitude and our actions. I blew this one in both those areas. I can't control what someone else thinks about me or my son. I can't change their minds or make them like me more or less. I should have taken the high road, smiled and said, "Yes, he sure didn't have very good sportsmanship tonight." Even if we don't get along with other parents, continue to be respectful, or at minimum, civil. Being civil to other parents can be especially difficult at times when we let our emotions boil over. My behavior was often borderline abusive to many parents, but fortunately, I never got into a physical altercation. I did however, observe one. It was yet another highly intensive AAA summer tournament, and it wasn't just the 90 degree heat that was causing issues! The competition between the parents and players in this particular tournament was extreme from puck drop. Shortly after the second period began, I heard yelling and screaming. I turned my head and witnessed a scuffle. Bodies were bouncing around, punches being thrown, and blood…. yes, blood at a YOUTH HOCKEY GAME! I was just grateful it wasn't me! There were two dads in full fist-to-cuffs, and I recognized them both. Both were great friends of mine. This happens a lot more than we hear about in the news. We only hear about the ones that involve players, or catastrophic outcomes. The sad thing is that both of these dads felt horrible afterward, and I'm sure visiting the local police department was humbling and embarrassing. This was an especially difficult situation for the players of these dads. We must attempt to control our emotions, no matter what it takes.

Remember, it's not about us; it's about the players and the team. Try and be friendly to all parents on your player's team. Keep your opinions to yourself. Trust me, you will be glad you did! Think about the hockey team your player is on as being like a business. Be as professional as possible. If your player was truly a professional – how would you conduct yourself? Try and remember to keep it professional on all levels with other parents. Remember, politics and cliques, as well as treatment of referees will be a challenge, but just control what you can (your attitude and actions), and remind your players they can only control their attitude and work ethic. Trust the process! And, follow this commandment: Thou Shalt Remember Thou Art the Parent, Not the Child!

NOTES/ CHALLENGES/ GOALS

V. THOU SHALT FOCUS ON DEVELOPMENT
ABOVE TEAM SELECTION

One of the biggest stress factors for parents in youth hockey is dealing with the stress of try-outs. For myself and other crazy hockey parents, the nightmare scenario being their player placed on the "lesser" team. In Minnesota association hockey, there are usually the A, B or C teams, "A" being the top players in that age group. I know every year the tryout process was brutal for me. Yes, I said that, for me. I was never too concerned about my player. I just wanted to ensure he was healthy and well rested in order to give him a fair shot at the tryouts. When I found out when tryout was, we cleared the calendar! No visitors, no friends over, and NO FUN! When he was about seven years old, we had just finished the first day of tryouts. He came out of the locker room and was so excited. I was thinking that maybe he heard from the coaches already and it was good news. No such luck! He smiled and said, "Tommy is having some of the boys over for a sleep over tonight, and he asked me to stay!" He was so thrilled to be part of the small group of boys that were asked to attend. My blood pressure immediately sky rocketed. I said, "You can't stay there tonight, you have tryouts again tomorrow!" He said, "That's okay,

Mom, the other boys are staying too." I said, "You will be up all night, eating bad food and playing video games, and you know you won't play well tomorrow." His face dropped as all the color drained out of him. That cute smile had turned upside down into a frown. He said, "Okay, Mom, I'll tell him I can't." I told him he would happy that he didn't go as he would play a lot better tomorrow. It was just another manipulation move on my part. I was worrying about the outcome of the tryout rather than letting him be a kid. He was heartbroken, and I felt like I won! He was seven years old.

Yes, it was my mission to ensure my player ate well, got plenty of rest and abstained from all physical activity during tryouts. I was obsessed with my player doing well, and as the crazy, helicopter mom, it was my job to control the process. Believe me, I did everything I possibly could to put my player at an advantage, but my controlling behavior didn't always pay off. It seemed every year he was sick during the tryout period. I remember several years where he had a horrible cold during the tryout, and one year he had the flu! You would think the world was going to end! I called one of the evaluating coaches and told him my son had the flu and was running a temp. Of course, I asked him where he would land if he wasn't able to attend. He stated that they would do the best they could to evaluate him from previous seasons, but he might end up on a

THE TEN COMMANDMENTS FOR HOCKEY PARENTS

lesser team since they would not be able to judge where he should be. Well, I certainly couldn't allow that. He might end up on the B team instead of the A team, and that would be traumatic for both of us! So, I proceeded to get him up, showered, and pumped him full of Motrin. When I dropped him off, I told him, "Now you hustle out there! I know you don't feel well, but you can rest afterwards, give it all you got!" And he usually did. Poor kid was profusely sweating when he got off the ice, and actually did well. Looking back on my desperate behavior, I realize just how crazy and obsessed I really was. What was the worst thing that could have happened if he didn't tryout due to illness, or stayed up all night at a friend's house playing video games? Yes, he might not make the A team, but that simply wasn't good enough for me. Many youth hockey parents have the same opinions about tryouts and team selections. Now that I have been through the process, I can honestly say the team your player ends up on isn't important. What is most important is that he or she develops into a better player during the season, creates friendships, and HAS FUN! During youth hockey, I have seen players that made the A team, and yet, they did not have a productive season. Usually one of two things would happen. They didn't have the confidence to play at that level, so they played tight and worried, and this affected their game. I also saw players that were exuberant to make the team as a bubble player and never got to play much. In contrast, I have witnessed sad players and parents that didn't make the better team, but the player ended up ripping it up on the lesser team by racking up points, gaining confidence, making friendships, and loving every minute of it.

There is really a "sweet spot" when it comes to developing as a player in youth hockey. Having your player on a team where they are challenged, yet she or he has the confidence to climb that mountain. I believe that most youth hockey organizations and clubs do the best they can to place players on the right teams. Teams that will enable them to develop their skills, gain confidence and have fun! That being said, I realize that evaluations are not always fair, and often times, players end up on teams that are not best fit for their development. My point is that one year or even two years on the "wrong" team isn't going to prevent them from becoming the players that they are destined to become!

Watching players over the years has been fascinating for me. I have seen players that were absolutely the best players in their organizations as 10 year old's, but didn't play high school hockey. A friend's son did not make his high school team as a 16 year old, but years later, signed a pro contract! Yes, it's true that it can happen! When my son played AAA hockey in the summers, there were parents with their chests puffed out like their players were the next NHL stars. Many of those players, despite having the best training, coaching and tons of money invested into them, didn't play college hockey in any capacity. The moral to the story here is to stay excited and positive about your players regardless of what team they are on. Offer them love, support and encouragement. And remember to focus on what you can control - your attitude and actions - and urge your players to focus on their attitude and work ethic! Trust the process and follow this Commandment: Thou Shalt Focus on Development Above Team Selection.

NOTES/ CHALLENGES/ GOALS

.

VI. THOU SHALT BE HAPPY FOR OTHER PLAYERS' SUCCESSES

One of the toughest parts of youth hockey is watching other players excel and seeing your player struggle. After watching many players develop along the way, I can say with confidence that every player develops at different times. I have literally watched a player as a PeeWee take the puck down the ice and skate around every player on the ice to score multiple times a game. Yet that same player was mediocre in high school and never played college hockey. As parents, we need to realize that being jealous of other players doesn't help our player rise any higher. This, coming from the craziest of hockey moms who always compared my player to others and expected my player to be the star on every team! To say this behavior was toughest on my player is an understatement. If I could re-do my youth hockey journey, I certainly wouldn't act like a jealous kid. I would understand that regardless of the pace each player develops, all players are fundamentally good people and we should be happy and encouraging for all of them!

Criticizing other players almost always stems from jealousy. I am going to call this as I see it, and I have been on both ends of this spectrum. When my son was a youth player, he was mediocre at best, and as I watched the star players come out, my criticism became fierce. On a regular game day, I would sit with the masses scrutinizing the best players on the team. Our favorite complaint was, "He never passes the puck. He's a puck hog, and his dad is counting his points." Later on when my son was in high school, he became a better player and at that time, the tables turned. Although I was thrilled that his hard work began to pay off, both my son and I were constantly attacked. Parents that were my friends would tell me that such and such parent was talking about my son being lazy. There was a definite theme to their grievances. "He never back checks and constantly gives up goals." "He only knows how to score, and he will never play at the next level." Years later, a parent told me that a high school coach used my son's name to current players when he wanted to find an example for being lazy. It never ends, and as a parent, it is possible that you will be on both sides of the controversy at some point in your player's development. The reality here again is to focus on the two things you can as a parent- your attitude and your actions.

Thou shalt be happy for other players' successes; in other words...DO NOT CRITICIZE OTHER PLAYERS, NO MATTER WHAT YOU THINK! Think of it if you want, but shut up! This type of behavior has a tendency to come back in

THE TEN COMMANDMENTS FOR HOCKEY PARENTS

your face. Remember, all players and parents are inherently good. Give them the benefit of the doubt. Jealousy is a poison. If Johnny is the best player on the team, be complimentary toward Johnny and his parents. Yes, I realize it gets old when Johnny makes the winning goal for the tenth game of the season, and scores his eighth hat trick, but bite your tongue and be happy for him (or act like it)! When Johnny comes out of the locker room and is surrounded by his smiling, proud parents and his posse, go up to him, in front of your player, and say, "Great game Johnny, I really love watching you play!" I know, I know, I never did that... but I should have. I wish I would have. Instead, I was the parent who was in the corner with a couple of other moms saying, "Oh, that Johnny is such a selfish player, and none of the boys on the team even like him." DON'T DO IT! Take the high road. The best part about not criticizing other players is that your player is watching and listening, and this will help him or her understand how to behave, how to celebrate others, and how to work hard for what you want in life. Don't bring up Johnny, but if your son does, simply say, "Yes, Johnny is a great player, hard work pays off." "If you keep working hard, I believe you will continue to get better and better." During this time, take the opportunity to point out the strengths and talents that your player has. Tell your player he or she did a great job on the back check, or she or he had a great pass in the second period. Take note of what your player does right in the game so you can encourage him or her after the game. Remind your player that hockey is a team sport, and each player plays a role in a team victory.

Don't ever compare your player to another player! Again, it's okay to mention that Johnny had a good game, but then talk about other great plays or players during the game. Of course, as with all bad hockey parent behavior, I am sure there were many times that I compared my player to other players. By doing this, we are not building our player's confidence; we are building animosity toward other players. As parents, we must model the behavior we expect our child to buy into. I remember one particular drive home from a Squirt game, when my son got into the car, and burst into tears. As he sat next to me, his face became more flushed, his nose was running, and he was uncontrollably weeping. I couldn't imagine why he was so upset. He had a decent game. He wasn't the star, but he did his best. His effort was an A. As parents, when we see our players in pain, it is human nature to want to protect and defend them. During that short three minute exchange, my mind was flying about whose A_ _, I was going to go after. Finally he said, "I'm never gonna be as good of a player as Jack!" And more tears came! Jack was our best player and happened to be my best friends' son. I waited a minute and said, "It's okay Bud, Jack is an unbelievable player. He works really hard, and is so talented. I especially like how hard he works out there. But, you are a good player too, and if you keep working hard and keep a good attitude, I know you are gonna get better and better." By the time we got home, he had calmed down. As the story goes, he did get better. He and Jack were the best of friends all through youth hockey, and into high school. They are still friends today, and Jack's parents are still some of my best friends. Be careful how you talk about other players in front of your player. Focus on the positives of all players, and do not compare your player to other players. Remember to focus on your attitude and actions and encourage your player to focus on their attitude and work ethic. Once again, trust the process. And, follow this commandment: Thou Shalt Be Happy for Other Players' Successes.

NOTES/ CHALLENGES/ GOALS

VII. THOU SHALT AVOID FILING BANKRUPTCY

There is a plethora of studies and statistics available online regarding how many youth or high school hockey players proceed on to college or professional hockey. Most of the information out there certainly isn't positive for our rising hockey players longing to continue playing after high school. One study reads that less than 2% of high school athletes (1 in 54) go on to NCAA Division I schools. This particular statistic includes all sports, not just hockey. According to the NCAA website, In 2018 there were 4,199 players playing NCAA hockey and of those, around 6% were projected to make the jump from NCAA to professional. With all the bleak and negative numbers out there, why is it that we happily pull our wallets and credit cards out to pay for the mounting costs of hockey? I have also read extensive stories about parents filing bankruptcy, maxing out credit cards, and literally taking out second mortgages to finance their player's dreams. Let's cover a couple of quick points before I get into making financial decisions in youth hockey. One is, are you sure this is your player's dream, or is it your dream? Looking back, I can honestly say that it was my dream more than my player's for many years, especially in the beginning. He was really there to have fun and be with his friends. I was secretly hoping he would become a professional player someday. Initially, many young players are resistant to the game for many reasons, but eventually they should warm up to playing and love it. If they don't, that might be an indication that they just don't have that dream in their hearts. Secondly, as a parent, you should not take on extreme debt in order for your player to participate (that coming from someone who maxed out two credit cards during a 15 year period). The initial card was $20,000, and the other was $10,000. Keep in mind, there were other expenses unrelated to this debt as well. I was a single mom raising a hockey player in Minneapolis/ St. Paul, Minnesota and hockey was not cheap. Part of the issue for me was that my son didn't see his father and he did not contribute to us financially, therefore- I had one income and was often working three jobs. If I could rewind, I would have started a fund for his hockey or whatever sport he liked, and made a contribution from each paycheck. That would have helped tremendously. Best practice is to keep it all in perspective, especially our expectations. If we decide to spend $100,000 on our player's development, remember that it may lead nowhere. This is something we have to come to terms with early. Don't have an expectation that goes along with the money spent. This will prevent anger and frustration if the player quits or does not achieve a college scholarship or a pro contract.

You might be wondering, "How can a parent possibly go into debt from hockey?" It's not difficult, especially when you consider all the expenses related to hockey, as well as the years that parents are supporting their player. Let's start with the equipment costs. Players need a helmet, stick, breezers, gloves, elbow pads, knee pads, shoulder pads, skates and sticks. They will need a hockey bag, guard covers, under garments, etc. Younger players are much easier to manage as they are too young to be screaming for the expensive gear or brand name gear, but that is also changing. Get to know the closest used sporting goods or hockey store and become a regular customer there. Safety is the most important factor at this age, so having a good fitting helmet is important. As your player gets older, sticks become the most expensive items, along with skates. Used skates can be purchased until your player is a bit older. Later on, buying a pair of skates that fit their feet properly will become more important. Depending on the store, it is possible to find used equipment that is nearly new. As your player ages, logically the price of their equipment will increase. This wouldn't be as difficult except for the additional expenses that now come into play.

Depending on where you live, team fees can vary. If your

player is playing association hockey, these may be the least expensive rates. In some states, players belong to "clubs," and these expenses for the season seem even higher. Best estimation, playing during the regular season can cost $800-$5000 per player. Keep in mind, this does not include hotels, food, gas and basic travel expenses if your player participates in out of town tournaments. My player participated in Minnesota association hockey for most of his youth career, but then began playing AAA or Tier One hockey around age 10. Some players play in the AAA league all year around, and some just participate in the off season so to speak, meaning, spring and summer.

My player played in the AAA league all year, one year, and the expenses were unreal. The charge for the regular season was around $1500- $2000, and travel cost was easily $2500-$3000. This was years ago, so you can imagine how much those costs have inflated today. The biggest challenge with the AAA teams is that most of the tournaments are out of state, and often in Canada, and that can ramp up your credit card balance quickly. Many parents struggle with whether or not to put their player on AAA teams. Is this the key to their development? There just simply is no guarantee. For us, playing in the AAA pool in the spring and summer helped my player to develop more, and I felt, kept him focused and increased both our social circles. We met great people, and some are still my best friends today! Looking back, hockey was really the catalyst to all of my friendships, and when hockey was over, it was like a death for me. I didn't see a lot of my hockey friends much after the season was over, and that was extremely lonely for me. One of the questions I hear often is, "If I don't do ____, will my player do this?" Meaning, if I don't allow my player to play AAA hockey, will he or she still develop into a great player? My answer would be, if you can comfortably afford it- meaning the expenses won't put a huge financial strain onto your family, then, consider it. Also, will the travel and schedule negatively affect your family? If the answer is no, then it might be a good idea. Decisions about teams really have to be broken down into time and money. Again, many of these tournaments are out of state or out of country. Will that work for your employer? All questions should be considered before saying yes to a team. The bottom line is, if your player is not able to participate, I believe, he or she will still become the player he or she was meant to be. Another option is to try the AAA route for a spring and summer, and assess how it goes with the travel, the cost, the time commitment, and go from there.

A few other expenses that may creep in as your child ages

are hockey camps, skating coaches and skill development sessions. I guess all of these could be put into the same category... possible bankruptcy. All joking aside, I believe that depending on the camp and coach, all of these methods can help your player develop and become better. The question once again becomes, "Is it financially and feasible for your family's player to participate?" We have a family friend who was convinced that his son was going to become a division one hockey player at minimum, if not a pro player. Because he wasn't happy with the development and coaching his son received during the regular season, every summer he spent literally thousands of dollars on additional developmental opportunities for his son. He enrolled him in several Elite hockey camps which cost thousands per camp, and also paid for private skill sessions with the coaches during these camps. The son had a mediocre high school season, followed by two years on a Junior Tier II team, and finally quit after being unsuccessful in garnering a college scholarship. Is it possible that going the extra mile for your player will indeed get them to the promised land? Of course it is possible. I have seen that happen as well, but it's not worth filing bankruptcy, or literally ruining your marriage over. Plus, many players have siblings, and having the family activities and spending revolve around Johnny's hockey isn't fair nor good for the entire family. The best words I can suggest are consideration, justification and moderation. Be sure that the development you are considering is indeed worth the money, be sure you can afford the money, and choose wisely!

One concept in hockey development training is that repetition of drills will lead to a mastering of skill development. In other words, if your player completes 10,000 hours of skill development, he or she will indeed become a master. If this was guaranteed, that would be great, but again, there are no guarantees in hockey. This concept certainly does not take into account the player's natural gifts and abilities. This could be a way to the poor house much quicker. Generally speaking, I do believe skill set repetition will indeed help your player improve, but how much? And, will this improvement assure them certain team selection, all-star status, college scholarships or an NHL contract? I am going to come back to the basic premise of this book which is that parents can control only their attitude and actions, and players can control their attitude and work ethic. Making financial decisions is difficult, but we can only do the best we can. Remember, if you have some type of expectation attached to those financial decisions you may end up disappointed. If you can simply support your player, and not expect anything while living within the confines of your finances and family, you will be able to enjoy watching your player be stress free and happy! Remember to follow this Commandment: Thou Shalt Avoid Filing Bankruptcy!

NOTES/ CHALLENGES/ GOALS

VIII. THOU SHALT FOLLOW THE HOCKEY PARENT PRINCIPLES

Being a good hockey parent is similar to being good at your career of choice. In this chapter, I am going to highlight what I call, "hockey parent principles." These are similar to a job description, with duties and responsibilities sprinkled in. Best practices that I can share with you, knowing that I wasn't good at any of these. Perhaps you can learn from me! When in doubt, refer back to these principles.

LET GO- Have you heard that saying, "Kids will be kids?" Well, I will expand on that a bit and say, "hockey kids will be hockey kids." Our players are going to make mistakes as they get acclimated to the game they love. As parents we need to let go and allow them to make those mistakes. I was the epitome of the helicopter hockey mom. My son started playing at age four, and yes at that age we need to put their gear on them, tie their skates and carry their bag. But, in a couple years, they should be starting to master these tasks on their own. My problem was, I didn't allow that to happen. I would go into the locker room, and help him. As I reflect now, it's pretty embarrassing, but I just couldn't let go and allow my player to deal with the challenges and struggles that often occur in the beginning years of hockey. My controlling behavior was all fine until he was a squirt, then I wasn't able to help him. Coaches would encourage the players to tie their own skates and put their own gear on. I was that mom that hung out outside the locker room so when it cleared out, I could go in and tie my son's skates and check all his gear! At one point, one of the coaches told me, "It is okay; if his skates are tight enough, he'll be fine." I was horrified! My baby could fall down or trip over a lace; the coach simply didn't know what he was talking about. I thought, "Easy for him, it's not his kid out there." Watching my son skate around with his skates clearly not tight enough absolutely killed me! During games, the coaches would help tie them if they were unusually loose. This process brought me many gray hairs and stress, but I got through it and eventually he was a master at it at age 21! Well, it would have been 21 if I had not had fellow parents and coaches counseling me through the process of letting go. It seemed that players with older siblings were much more seasoned and independent. The coaches also caught me carrying my player's bag. His bag literally weighed more than he did. One of the coaches made a comment once, and I barked back, "The bag weighs more than he does." He said, "Then, get one with wheels," so we did. Today, some teams do not allow bags with wheels. It really depends on the level of the team and the league.

Another issue I had was hanging around the rink when my player was practicing. Yes, I was one of two, often the only parent at the rink. It was 6am on a Saturday, and I would drop my player off at the front entrance, only to park the car, grab my coffee and blanket and head inside. Looking back, my player had to be somewhat embarrassed that his parent was one of the crazies sitting in the stands freezing to death watching practice. Other parents would pull up and pick up their player afterwards, and would see me walking out of the rink. They would say, "You didn't sit in the rink all practice, did you?" I proudly replied, "Yes, I did!" I would study the coaches, other players, and of course- my little NHL player in the making! Letting go is really an important part of the youth hockey journey. Trusting the process, and allowing the coaches to do what is best for your player. Also, trust your player. If there is an issue, they will likely tell you about it, if not, the coach will. No need to freeze to death in the rink. Better yet, use that hour or so to do something for yourself. In later years, I would use that time to walk. I scoped out all the walking trails around the practice rinks, and went to work! I felt amazing and refreshed just in time for the pick up!

EXPOSE YOUR PLAYER TO OTHER THINGS- I know parents that have told me their player loved hockey from the age of two, and never played anything else. By high school, my son had also become exclusive athlete to the sport of hockey, but I was sure glad I encouraged him to try other sports and activities. My player played baseball, lacrosse, basketball and dance! Yep, I took him to a dance class when he was about five years old. I was so excited for him to experience the dancing and music. As I dropped him off, I was thinking, "Dance might really be his thing." To this day, I have no idea what happened in that room, but when I arrived to pick him up, the teacher couldn't wait to get rid of him. I excitedly asked, "How did it go?" She said, "Well, let's put it this way- I don't think dance is for him." She was tight lipped on any other details. Predictably, I grilled him on the way home. He didn't say anything except he didn't like it, but why did I have the distinct idea that he probably made that poor teacher's life hell that day? I realize that as our players age, there is another huge controversy about whether or not they should quit other sports and pick one sport as they prepare for college. That is a decision that only parents and their players can make, and each player's school, family and situation are different. I would say in grade school, exposure to multiple sports and activities can only be positive. Looking back on our situation, my player was giving it a valiant effort with a three sport focus going into his sophomore year. That was until he started experiencing hip pain. After an examination, x-rays, and discussion, the doctor recommended he cut something out of his busy physical schedule. At that time he was playing hockey twelve months a year, playing soccer in the fall (which also required miles of running), and Lacrosse in the spring. The doctor simply said he was overusing his hips, and he would be a likely candidate for a hip replacement at some point in the future. You may know of hockey goalies that have had both of their hips replaced by age 18 -- it's crazy! These athletes are beating up their bodies fast and furious, especially when sports becomes much more demanding in the high school years. The decisions on what to play or not play become more difficult later, but for young athletes it's often best to expose them to a variety of activities and sports, and let them decide what they like best. My player recently has re-discovered his love for baseball, even though he hasn't played in years. He told me that he wishes he would have played in high school. I felt bad about that, but I feel like we made the best decision we could at the time considering schedules, family time, his physical issues and his year round commitment to hockey. All we can do is gather information and make the best decisions we can at that time, and let it go.

PROVIDE EMOTIONAL SUPPORT- I alluded to the importance of not acting like the coach for your player. Much of this has to do with you being the parent to them, and providing that much-needed emotional support. Our players need a safe place to go. Oftentimes, they get frustrated with other players, their coaches, playing time and more. We need to be there for them to vent, and just listen. The one mistake I made many times was trying to be my usual "super fix it mom." Any time my player was upset, I went to work immediately on fixing the problem, or issue, for him. This is not always a good idea since the coach doesn't appreciate Johnny running home and telling mom he was mean to him at practice. Then mom calls the coach and chews him out. Ultimately, Johnny goes to practice and gets the cold shoulder from the coach. This can affect playing time, trust, and other aspects that coaches find important. I had a laundry list of this type of behavior. After my player figured it out, he would start saying, "Mom, don't say anything, but ….." That didn't always shut me up either. Bottom line is that our players need us to be sounding boards, confidantes, partners, therapists and support systems. If they tell us to keep something quiet, we have to! That is really what emotional support is all about. Being there for them unconditionally and attempting to be a good listener. Try and stay positive, and remind them they can only control two things: their attitude and work ethic. We should focus on the two things we can control …our attitude and actions. Trust the process!

IT'S ABOUT THEM- NOT YOU! - This is an area that I simply failed in over and over again. I was always concerned about what people would think if my player made the lesser team, got into trouble during a game, wasn't the top scorer on the team, etc. The strange thing was I had myself convinced that everything I did was to protect, or help my player. I was self-brainwashed. The fact was that I was focused on myself, not my player. Once, when my player was a Pee Wee, he went to check another player, clearly not knowing what he was doing and checked him from behind. I was horrified!! I do believe he was learning the actual method of properly checking, but nonetheless he was suspended for a game. I was so embarrassed and angry. After he got undressed and came out of the locker room, I gave him the dirtiest look. We got into the car and I proceeded to rail on him. If I would have looked closer, I would have noticed he felt bad enough and he was confused. He was trying to play aggressively and was sure he didn't mean to hurt the other player. Thank God the other player was fine, but again, I made this about my embarrassment, and not about him. I should have been asking myself, "How can I support him?" Asking questions like, "Are you okay? Is there something I can do to help? Do you want to talk about it?" Keeping it about the players, not us, is truly an important part of the hockey parent job description.

My player's hockey journey also became my social journey, dictating my friends and social circles. My best friends were the parents on our team, and I was always the vicious gang leader of our parent group. I didn't have a lot of respect for any parent or child that my posse didn't like. I couldn't wait for the pre and post-game party activities. I would be the first one there, and the last to leave, even if I missed some of the game. Out of town tournaments were truly when I was on my worst behavior, such as staying up half the night, drinking and partying, while my player slept in the room. Huge hangovers and impatience the next day as my selfishness took center stage. With my boozing came more bad behavior. One season, I had a huge crush on our coach! Yes, I did, and it was the focus of my life and the season. This particular coach was single, but had a live-in girlfriend. I partied with him as much as I could at away tournaments, hoping he would come around. Well, he didn't. As a result, some parents and kids on the team figured it out, and starting talking about my son getting special treatment from the coaches. That year, my player was named Captain, and a

huge implosion occurred with the team and the parents. My
son was devastated by it, yet I didn't realize, nor care. In the
end, he never left his girlfriend. He's still with her today. In
retrospect, he really had no intention of dating me; he was just
having fun, I got all sucked into it, and again- my player
suffered as a result. I have seen a lot of this on the hockey trips
-- infidelity between coaches and moms, and parents, cheating.
I am not perfect, but I sure wish I would have done a better job
keeping it about my player, and not me!

HELP YOUR PLAYER STAY HEALTHY- This was a
concept that I caught on to very late in my player's
development. I was the busy mom that was going to the
McDonald's and Culver's drive up for dinner, and feeding my
son chicken fingers for five meals a week! Today, as a health
coach, it's horrifying to think of the bad food we both
consumed. I need to point out that I do believe in moderation
here too. I don't necessarily believe that every young hockey
player should be abstaining from carbs, sugar and dairy! I do
believe that we can encourage our players to eat healthy, and
urge them to understand that what they eat actually fuels their
bodies. Meaning, if they want to have good energy for a game,
eating a healthy meal or snack is going to give them that boost,
as opposed to drinking pop, eating ice cream, or French fries.

Today's coaches and parents do a much better job educating their players and parents about nutrition and how good nutrition plays a role in having a successful season. Because I was late on understanding this concept, my son was extremely overweight by age 10.

During his first AAA experience, the team actually had a player profile book. Looking through it, all the other boys looked the same, thin and healthy. My son stuck out like a sore thumb. He looked like a poster child for Dunkin Donuts! I can say that now because we both laugh about it all the time, and I still have that profile book. The extra weight on his frame, and his lack of healthy eating habits took its toll that year. Early in the season, the coach made it clear that he needed to lose weight, and he was very truthful about that. I tried to help my son make better choices and did all I could to help him cut weight in preparation for team selections for a big tournament in Canada. The day the coach was meeting with the players, I was so nervous for my son. I dropped him off at the rink and said a little prayer for him. He had been doing well at practice and working hard on losing weight. When I picked him up a couple hours later and as he got into the car, I could tell it wasn't good news. After driving about one block, he burst into tears. It was like a dam broke, and the water started rushing out of his eyes. He said the coach told him he was still too heavy and needed to lose 7-10 pounds. He also said that his weight was preventing him from having the stamina to keep up with the other kids. I was so angry! Without a few minutes of thought on how to proceed, I grabbed my phone and called the coach. He was very nice about it, but really he had a myriad of players that he could choose from, and my son didn't fit the mold. He was probably right about his weight, but seeing my son in all that pain made me realize he wasn't getting any more confident- he was just feeling degraded. We talked, and he finished out the year, but didn't go back to that team. The next year, he ended up on another team he loved! He thrived on this team because the coaches believed in his talent, despite his weight issues. Years later, the extra weight came off, as we both became more educated about good nutrition. Finding a balance is really the key here, especially since they are kids. We don't want to become the drill sergeant for nutrition, nor the mini-doughnut mom! I have observed parents going overboard with the healthy food and snacks, not allowing their players any treat time. Eventually, these kids will sneak food, and binge on bad foods. This can create a negative relationship with food. It's really important to educate our players on healthy eating and nutrition. The WHY's of food. The Fuel vs Poison. Discussing how good foods going in will create the energy they need to play well. In contrast, how bad foods like sugar can cause them to crash, and prevent their bodies from working at full capacity. Balance and education are the keys!

THE LIFE LESSONS OF HOCKEY- I believe as parents, we can use the game of hockey to teach our players many important aspects of life. Hard work is a concept that hockey teaches that we can tie info our everyday lives, especially as adults. The idea that putting in a solid effort will indeed pay off! My dad would always say, "You get out of it what you put into it." We can encourage our players that if you put the time in, you will become a better player, and will be one step closer to your goals and dreams! This idea also directly ties into the belief in oneself. Our players often deal with disappointments and adversity. As parents, we can be honest by telling them they will deal with these same types of issues as adults. Encouraging them to never give up, and never doubt themselves. Disappointments can lead to wonderful things, and true character building. When a player doesn't make the team they wanted to make, it might just end up for the better. A player on a lesser team may start out the season disappointed but eventually realize he or she has grown as a player through more ice time and development opportunities. This will in turn, help his or her confidence to sky rocket. Each one of our players is special and unique. Each one has talents that are remarkable and outstanding. Try and point those out while focusing on staying positive in all they do! Hockey also produces some of our players' greatest friendships. My older sister always told me that no matter what the cost of hockey, keep my player in it as long as possible because it will dictate his friends, and keep him busy. Looking back, I believe that. Many kids are bored, and that can cause them to take up with the wrong crowd or get into trouble. Most weekends, and some week nights, we were busy. Often, the hockey led to sleep overs, and other activities. Because hockey is a team sport, team work is also a life lesson of the game of hockey. You win and lose as a team! That is a statement that hockey families repeat and believe in! Hockey is a game of team work, and I have seen some incredible passing plays that have truly led to the greatest of wins! We can teach our players that passing the puck to a teammate is just as important as scoring the winning goal! It's team work! Every player on the team has a role to play; therefore, every player is part of that team! My son always had a tough time with that one. He was often the king of assists, but rarely scored a goal. One season, one of our coaches could see this was getting him down. He came in with a printed sheet, and handed it to my son. It was a copy of all of Wayne Gretzky's stats. Now, you would think that "THE

GREAT ONE," was the king of burying the biscuit when in fact- he had more assists than goals. This was a huge lift for my son! He realized that assists and team work were just as important as goal scoring!

Finally, and most importantly, communication is a key skill learned in hockey that translates into life. Imagine that an adult wants a raise from his current employer. He's been working extremely hard and helping the company's production increase on a daily basis, but he's not happy with his paychecks. How would he approach his boss and ask for a raise? Could he do it? What would he say? These are all issues that our players will deal with in hockey. My son struggled the most with talking to the coaches. When he was upset about something, I would encourage him to talk to the coaches about it. This was extremely difficult for him. (Perhaps that is why I kept bothering them). He was shy and scared. Because he didn't have a dad in his life, he seemed even more fearful of approaching the coaches. The good news is he did get better at this because he had to. Most of the time, coaches aren't going to approach every player and ask if they need to talk or have any concerns. Our players must learn how to put their fears aside and communicate, and for some players this is very difficult. Participating in hockey encourages them to do that, along with building trust with their coaches and other players on the team. Verbal communication was not my player's only issue; he also had a major problem with his non-verbal communication. From a very early age, his frustration during a game became blatantly clear, and the coaches attempted to address it. He would shrug his shoulders on the ice when he was upset with a bad call, or smack his stick on the ice. Referees could see this behavior as well as other parents. My player constantly struggled with this, but became more aware of it and was controlling it by high school age. Along with the non-verbal's came the emotional outbursts! Hockey is an emotional game. Look at the parents! We all scream and yell, and act like idiots in the heat of the game; for our players, this can be worse! As our players age, emotional outbursts become less tolerable during games, and eventually lead to penalties. This can cause a loss for the team. As our players' age and get into the "real world", they also must control their emotions. As much as we don't like our bosses, we can't freak out at them, or lose our tempers. Controlling non-verbal and verbal communication during youth hockey can truly lead our players to being better at those skills as adults.

Looking back on our experience with youth hockey, I truly believe the game has brought my player many life lessons and helped improve social skills! As parents, we should have also learned those lessons. We can only control two things: our attitude and our actions. Our player can control their attitude and work ethic. Relax, take a deep breath, and trust the process! Follow this Commandment- Thou Shalt Follow the Hockey Parent Principles.

NOTES/ CHALLENGES/ GOALS

IX. THOU SHALT TRUST GOD AND THE PROCESS

What does the word "trust" actually mean? Merriam Webster's definition is: "assured reliance on the character, ability, strength, or truth of someone or something." The word "Process" is defined as a natural phenomenon marked by gradual changes that lead toward a particular result. As parents, we do not know what that result will be. Will the end result of our youth hockey journey be our youth players ending their season without playing again? Or will the end result be our players signing a professional hockey contract? It is likely that the end result will be somewhere in between. There is simply no way of knowing, and we should know that. However, we can't control the end result of all the time, emotional support, training, patience, love, and money we put toward our player's hockey journey. When we sign our players up for hockey, we take a step of faith. We hope they have fun and get better- not knowing the final outcome. In the beginning, we put our faith in the coaches, and we are committed to trust the process. Why is that this belief changes over time?

I'm going to ask you to step into my time machine! Yes, I have one, and I want you to come onboard. I am going to take you back to the year you first signed up your players for hockey. They are four, five, seven, maybe ten years old. You are likely thinner with less gray hair. You definitely have fewer wrinkles because your hockey induced stress anxiety is in your future. What happened? Back then, the feeling is light and playful. Your player is standing in line, flushed face, smiling. He or she is about to get on the ice for the first time. Both you and your player are beaming with excitement and anticipation. Perhaps you are thinking about your player making the NHL someday, but I doubt that. You are probably hoping he or she will have fun, meet new friends and get better as a player. As the years roll on, we become jaded. Jealous of other players that stand out, angry at the coaches for not playing our players enough, discontented with the organization and butting heads with other parents. As our expectations rise, so does the chaos and bad behavior. The fun of the game is like a fleeting shadow... long gone! There is a saying that I like to use, "Blessed are those who expect nothing, for they shall not be disappointed." I am not saying to work to give your player opportunities, help them make good decisions, and work toward their dreams- I'm saying not to expect that things will always turn out the way you want. As with life, hockey has its ups and downs, its challenges, disappointments. Trust the process.

In order to trust the process, we need to stop worrying, stop talking and stop controlling! Wouldn't it be amazing if we, as parents, could focus on being better listeners than talkers? Listening is a skill. I can honestly disclose that during the youth hockey journey, I was not a good listener. Listening is defined as giving one's attention to sound or action. Listening is an important part of effective communication. If we do not listen effectively, messages are misunderstood, meaning, we aren't really understanding our player's needs or wants. Our listening skill can be improved by being attentive and relaxed, and keeping an open mind. Understanding is part of the listening process and one that we all could improve. If we are truly listening, we will be tuned into our players, knowing if something isn't right for them, there will be signs. By listening, rather than talking, we will be better able to understand those needs. If I could do it all over again, I would stay positive, encourage, and not criticize, and listen rather than speak. Most important, I would let my player take the lead. If players want to talk, they will start the conversation. At that point, I would listen better, and answer accordingly. Learn from my mistakes!

Another element that is important in trusting the process is believing that there will be the right people there to help our players along. Because I was a single mom, it was important for me to have another male role model that my son could talk to. And, by the grace of God, we always had someone! Sometimes it was another dad, another coach, or a family friend, but there was always someone. Throughout this process of playing and learning the game, your player is learning coping skills, communication skills, team work skills and so many other Life Lessons! Hockey is not perfect, and neither is life. How the players learn to cope with difficulties on the hockey stage can translate into helping them cope with life's issues and problems. Remember, even if you are a parent coach, be open to other individuals helping your child. Listen, allow feedback, and be grateful.

As I am wrapping up the final chapter of this book, I want to go back to my love of the game of hockey, and the person who really loved the game before me: my dad. He has been an inspiration, and through watching his love of the game I have grown to love the game over the years. My dad is a man of great wisdom, and during my panicked years of youth hockey, while I was trying to control every part of my player's experience, his words rang true then, and still ring true today. One of his favorite sayings was, "If they love the game, they'll be good at it." That might not seem like a mind altering profound statement, but it is. This is yet another component of trusting the process. He was saying that hard work does pay off, and if our players truly love the game of hockey, they will seek out help they need, and they will do whatever it takes to get better. This also comes back to our players focusing on the two things they can control: their attitude and work ethic. We must believe that as parents, we can't make it happen for our players; all we can do is the very best we can. Use our common sense and knowledge to make the best decisions about their development choices, teams, equipment, schedules, etc. Once that is done, they are on their own, and if they really love this amazing game, they will put forth the extra added effort it takes to play at the next level. This reminds me of an interview I watched once on television. The man that was being interviewed was credited for helping a group of young African American males turn their academic achievements around. He told of how he met with the group and told them this, "It's easy to be ordinary, but it's difficult to be extraordinary. If you want to be 'extraordinary' you have to look at the word and break it down. It is made up of two words, 'extra' and 'ordinary.'" He went on to say, "If you want to be extraordinary, you have to do the 'extra' stuff." That hit home for me, and I have told that story many times to players, parents, and also to students I have taught at the college level. This rings true in many areas of life. If our players love the game, they'll willingly do the extra stuff, whatever it takes to become extraordinary!

The other statement that my dad would say came during a time when I was struggling with choosing a high school for my son. I was going back and forth on public or private. This school had better hockey coaches. This other school had a better overall program. Then there was the academic evaluation of each school and where his friends were playing. Upon watching me agonize over this decision for a couple years, my dad said this, "If you are good, they'll find you." I asked what he was talking about. He went to describe how good players are always found by someone. Someone important will see them play- a scout, coach, parent. Opportunities at the next level will come. Again, trust the process!

Multiple studies have shown that the #1 reason kids participate in sports is to have fun! Winning and attaining scholarships or NHL contracts didn't make the cut on any of these surveys. Our players simply want to have fun, and as parents we should be asking ourselves this important question, "What are we doing to be sure they are having fun?" Instead, we are complaining about the coaches, the lack of ice time, the other players, the other parents, or just about anything that is negative. If we put the focus back into the fun, I believe our kids will follow suit. If they are having fun, chances are they will get better at whatever they choose to be a part of. Remember, as parents we can control two things: our attitude and our actions, and follow this Commandment- Thou Shalt Trust God and the Process.

NOTES/ CHALLENGES/ GOALS

IX. THOU SHALT FOLLOW ADVICE FROM THE MASSES

Yes, I believe we can learn from those who preceded us in this amazing journey! The following chapter is dedicated to friends and acquaintances who have already walked in your shoes. They have willingly written both short and long pieces of advice for you! Some of them have players who ended their hockey careers after youth hockey, and some have players playing at the highest levels today- the National Hockey League! One thing I believe all of them have in common is a desire to share their knowledge and expertise! ENJOY!

Don't critique your child's performance immediately after a game. If your child wants your opinion, they will ask for it. Too many times, I believe a parent thinks they are doing their child a favor by telling them what they did wrong, they are not... Be supportive.

Let them have fun! There should be no pressure to be the best as someone will always be better. Realize the chance of your player going pro is nil. Have fun with parents, and don't compete against each other's players. These parents will be with you a lot and could be lifetime friends. The sport is very spendy, especially if they play all year around, but it's all worth it. You always know where your players are every night of the week!

Build the rink, let the kids come over, buy the hot chocolate and kick back. I have pictures of at least 40 pairs of skates and 40 sticks scattered in our 8 x 10 back hall way and I would give anything to have those days back. It was work and when you are in it it's stressful, but relish the moments. If your kid continues to work, it will pay off. Just stay out of it and let them pave their own road. Coaches can suck and so can other parents, welcome to life. Sports can teach you and your child a lot from work ethic, healthy eating habits, team work, perseverance, and hard lessons like even if you work your hardest it may not work out. How many times can you get knocked down and get back up? That depends on attitude, and you as a parent can help shape that attitude by how you react to your child's hockey experience. Don't wreck it for your kid. Everyone knows who the crazy parents are; don't be that parent! You are not helping your kid. The game of hockey belongs to the kids, be the role model that makes that happen and volunteer your time if those are your beliefs in order to help foster an ethical honest program wherever you are.

Kids will all develop at different ages. If your child does not make the AA team or the youth all-star team, don't worry. I have seen kids who were considered some of the best hockey players in their age group in youth hockey never play one game of high school hockey for various reasons. I have also seen kids that played B hockey become very good high school and even college players. I would rather have my child play B hockey and get a ton of ice time then play AA hockey and only see the ice a few times a game.

Development should be dictated largely by the player. If you can't drag them off the ice that's one thing, but if the child wants to play baseball or go to the beach- don't force them to practice. Like the games themselves, development should be fun. Don't buy into the B.S. like 3:1 practice to game ratio. Playing games is often the best development. Obviously skating is important, but if a kid is truly passionate about hockey then they will WANT to skate like Crosby and even the line drills won't be a chore.

Parents- please understand that it is just a game, and although it can get pretty intense at times, parents need to put it in perspective. To me, youth sports are one of the best ways to learn life lessons for kids, but parents have to make sure to allow their kids to learn those lessons without getting too involved. Parents shut up and let your kids play! Parents should cheer, coaches should coach, kids should play….. repeat if necessary!

Biggest mistake I saw many parents make was imposing their own passion on their kids. Soon as the kid got old enough, he quit. Experts call that burnout, but it's not. There is no such thing as burnout in hockey. If a kid is truly passionate, he doesn't burn out. They only quit when they are being forced into it in the first place.

Be supportive of your player, give them your love, and then stay out of the way. A parent may disagree with coaches at times, but as long as there is no physical or verbal abuse that your child is going through, let the coaches coach and the kids play.

For parents just starting out, I would say keep it fun! Make sure hockey is THEIR passion and not yours. If it's truly their passion then cost should not be an issue so long as you can afford it. Never lose sight that it's a game, not a job. It should be fun!

Don't rush it! Relax and enjoy the experience! It goes by too fast! Try and not get caught up in all the hockey craziness. Your player needs to have fun!

Never look further ahead than the level they are playing at. I had one parent tell me their kid was NHL material (at the Pewee level) and they were skipping college to move to Canada. He played only Division 3. He was under tremendous pressure all those years.

Don't pressure your kid. He must play for himself, not you- the parent. If your hockey player has the passion, then you as the parent can provide them the opportunity to succeed.

Would I do it all again? Yes, but I would do it differently. I would have taken my family trips. My biggest regret is believing that you have to be "all in". Truth is, you do, but in the end the politics play way more than you think into hockey. So, dedicate your family to the sport and have fun, but do not let it take over your family. You can take the trip; if your kid is good he will play, one week away shouldn't deter from that. If it does, switch programs. We did a good job balancing but we could have done better. The kids will be as good as the parents. You get what you give.

Parents should NOT offer advice regarding how their player should play. It will destroy all the coach is trying to teach. At the squirt level, I had one parent offering her player money to score goals. Hockey is a team sport and what the parent did was selfish and destructive to the team.

As a parent- be their biggest fan, not their coach! Be positive, not critical. Don't offer advice and discuss your player's games, only if they ask. Do not criticize your players' teammates or coaches. Being negative spreads like a disease!

My best advice is to not rush it, relax and enjoy the experience! It all goes by so fast. And don't get caught up in the craziness of youth hockey. Most importantly, your child needs to have fun!

As a mom, you need to learn to be ready at all times. That means having cash for concessions at all times. I always kept a $20, a helmet kit and extra laces in the console of my car. I can't tell you how many times I had to use it! I also would keep at least two blankets and a fleece jacket in my car year round. Summer hockey is the worst if you walk in with shorts and a tank to watch your kid play and you have nothing warm to wrap around you! Again, I can't tell you how many times when they were younger I shivered until I learned to be prepared. When I had younger kids, I kept a small bag with things to do in the car as well. These special items could only be used at hockey.

Playing sports is about the kids not the adults. Adult fun is secondary to making sure the kids are having fun. Out of town tournaments should be about the life lessons and team community.

Parents need to have a long-term approach with a soft hand on their child's development. Avoid an intensive development plan including rigorous meal plan, lifting weights and constant repetition. Losing games is the best life-long learning. You don't always have to win!

There is no need to break the bank on all the expensive equipment available, just make sure things fit to avoid injury.

Family is more than just running kids to games and practices. Include family trips, visits with relatives and even Sunday dinners.

Referees, umpires and other youth sports volunteers are not your enemy. These people are not professionals and will make a lot of mistakes. Instead of criticizing, jump in and help, support them and be positive. Your athletes will appreciate your behavior.

Understand your child's real abilities. If they are strong players, they probably will be playing. The true problem seems to be the player that is on the bubble and may not be in the right level of play.

Expect your child will not receive a scholarship.

Trust the coach's processes. Believe that he/she has a plan in the best interest of the team and each individual. If you have questions or concerns, do not complain to other parents, critique or criticize from the stands, during social events or on social media. Go directly to the coach and ask your questions or explain your concerns. Coaches care deeply about each individual as the success of the team and season is dependent on building a strong culture within the locker room and instilling the belief that each athlete plays an important role.

Allow your athlete the opportunity to play several sports. Developing athletic movement patterns from different sports builds overall athleticism, keeps motivation and enthusiasm high and better prepares the athlete for advanced and progressive developmental plans.

Do not car coach your athlete before or after games, practices and competitive events. Ask questions, provide supportive feedback and encourage them. Never criticize them for their performance; they know when they under-performed and do not need negative reinforcement. Remember that their brain continues to form and develop well into their 20's. They will internalize your feedback both negative and positive to create their identity and feeling of self-worth and value. Be a part of building a positive image and instilling self-confidence.

Don't tell your child to do something the way you think it should be done instead of how the coach wants it done.

Always... Keep your mouth shut!

If your player wants to be a goalie - let him/her be a goalie. They are a special breed with a unique passion that will take them far in life well beyond their time in hockey.

Enjoy every minute! Late night practices, pasta feeds, tournaments, early morning practices! This time with your kids goes by so fast! Take it all in! Some of my favorite moments were driving my son to and from practices and games!!!

Well, my advice would be just to be there for your player emotionally, physically and mentally. Be their number 1 fan. Stay out of the chaos from other parents and players. Have a BIG pocket book and enjoy the ride because it goes by in the blink of an eye.

Just because you start this ride doesn't mean you get to stop it or keep it going for your player. They say when it ends, you don't. And, that can be the hardest part.

Help them to become more independent, but it doesn't hurt to check all your equipment before leaving town for a tournament or game! Hard to play hockey on one skate!

Enjoy the ride. Do NOT have any preconceived expectations. They will ruin your trip!

The people in your association or club are not out to get you or your player. Don't take it personally if your player doesn't make the top team every year. It happens, and maybe they are right where they belong.

Let the coaches coach. In the younger years they are mostly volunteers and they are doing their best. As far as when they start tryouts for teams, I have heard its politics and sometimes it may be, but hard work and skill beat that. Coaches want to win games at the older levels and they will play who they see are working hard and reward them. Complaining will get you more time on the bench.

Never think that your player is the best one on the team. All kids develop at different times and some will catch up and pass others up. Making an A team isn't always the best thing either. If your player is playing 3rd line on an A team, they are better off on the B team- more playing time there! There were many happy parents whose players made the A team, only to complain when they weren't getting much playing time.

Parents need to keep their thoughts about other players on the team to themselves. Talking about other kids causes the kids to treat each other differently.

Enjoy every moment! The early mornings and the raw hands from tightening skate laces is a quick phase. Soon enough, they are driving themselves to the rink. Have fun cheering them on and seeing them improve.

Treasure the moments with fellow hockey parents in the stands. You will have an incredible bond as your kids progress through the years. We are so lucky to be hockey parents. Never forget that! Also, take a lot of pictures and videos! You won't regret it!

Youth hockey is a growing experience for kids and parents. Let the kids grow with it and take their lumps along the way! Don't try to pave the path in front of them. They will be stronger adults as a result. Make youth hockey memorable for all the RIGHT reasons!

Do not force the athlete if it is not their passion. If it is, they will ask for more ice time and lessons. You can offer the idea of additional training but let them decide. Also support the sport. It is expensive. Don't complain every time your athlete needs a new stick or pair of skates. Prepare financially for the costs. As they get older, the costs get higher.

Keep things in perspective when they're young superstars and can stick handle all the way down the ice and score. Once checking is introduced, that ends. Also, if your player is scoring 3, 4 or 5 points a game, they're not at the right level of competition.

Your children should be playing the sport for themselves. Don't live vicariously through the eyes of your children. Your childhood is over. Support them when they play well and analyze, not scream, when their effort is lacking. Ultimately, sports teach us life lessons and should be a stepping stone for what's ahead in the real world. The majority of athletes never play past high school.

Let the players, play, the coaches, coach, the referees, ref and the fans, cheer!

Know your child's limitations. Not all children are hockey players.

Be the best cheerleader in the crowd. Contagious energy to build the team up regardless of winning/losing. They'll laugh and pressure to perform will be gone, just good hockey! Team spirit!

I just can't emphasize enough the importance of good study habits and grades for any child who thinks they might want to play in college. Studying and good grades are a habit and hockey should never come first. So many more doors are open to a hockey player with good grades!!

I really believe that if a child is meant to play high school and then possibly college hockey, he or she will get there without obsessive focus on hockey.

Never worry that your young child didn't make the top team. All kids develop at different ages so just let them have fun and enjoy playing the sport they love! When older, if they are not happy with what team they make, they need to evaluate what they could do to improve. I tell my kids if you do extra outside of practice you will get better. You have to let them decide. If they love it they will do extra things to improve.

Surround yourself with people who are truly happy for your child. Once your child has success, you will know who his or her supporters are. They will be the best cheerleaders in the crowd with contagious energy to build the team up regardless of winning / losing. They'll laugh and the pressure to perform will be gone, just Good Hockey! Team Spirit!

Do what is best for your child. You don't have to be on a team that is a money maker or a big name. If your child truly has talent the right coaches will find your hockey player. The coaches will be able to see your child has the passion and grit to make it in the hockey world. It's really up to the player to reach their goal, not the parents.

I think it is important that these young athletes spend time on their academics first and sports second. Encourage, support, cheer, but don't let them get away with BS in the name of a sport.

If your player has a goal of making a certain team, and the only thing they got good at over the summer was video games, it's not the coaches fault for not picking them. Nobody is going to give it to them. It has to be worked for. Hard work beats talent when talent doesn't work hard.

Never discuss the game during the car ride home or at the dinner table.

Hockey as a game is supposed to be fun! We have lost that with our kids all wanting to play at higher levels. As a youth hockey parent, try and keep the focus on fun and the rest will fall into place!

Some kids just aren't mean to play hockey past youth hockey and that's okay. I have seen parents on teams pushing their kids to work harder to get there. Some of them just don't want to, and as parents- we have to accept that.

Your player should be dressing themselves and tying their own skates by Squirt level. Try and encourage them to learn, and allow the coaches to help. At some point, parents have to stay out of the locker room!

If you have fun as a parent, your child will have fun! Stay light, even if it gets stressful!

The other day we found out a kid that used to be on our team has cancer. Wow, really put it all in perspective on so many levels. Hockey is a game. Life is life. Enjoy, and remember that there are more serious things that are happening than hockey.

GOD BLESS!!!!

NOTES/ CHALLENGES/ GOALS

AUTHOR BIOGRAPHY

Melissa West Versich is a veteran hockey mom that holds a Master's degree in Communication. She is also a certified Personal and Professional Life Coach who enjoys coaching other parents and individuals. Melissa also teaches Speech and Communication courses at the college level, and is a public speaker at both large and small events. Her most important life's work has been being the single mother of an aspiring hockey player. This hockey mom currently resides in "the state of hockey,"- Minnesota.

ADDITIONAL NOTES:

Made in the USA
Middletown, DE
12 February 2022